5/26/2019

Dear Cristophe!

These poems had a long
gestation. I do hope

Songs for Diana

that some of them speak
to you.

much love,

S tin

Songs for Diana

Poems by

Stanford Searl

Cover Art: Glenn Wong
of GW Graphic Works, Los Angeles, CA

ISBN: 978-1-949229-88-2

Kelsay Books Inc.

kelsaybooks.com

502 S 1040 E, A119
American Fork,Utah 84003

To Julia Anna Searl Rusert

Contents

Preface

Songs for Diana is a personal letter one might be lucky enough to receive from a close friend or confidant. At the very least it is a letter to be cherished. It staggers me each time I read these poems because they remind me of a letter I found in a suitcase among my mother's things, a letter I was unable to put down because it said so much about the past and my personal reality. I am also reminded of Marcus Aurelius' *Meditations* where Marcus writes, "You have power over your mind—not outside events. Realize this, and you will find strength." Searl finds strength in his vocation, a college professor in the rust belt, of all places, Buffalo, NY. He takes us through a most catastrophic event, the birth, life and early death of a severely retarded child, for which the pain still lingers, all in a city that hazes its inhabitants with snow, ice and howling wind. These epistles cry for connection, always compassionate and kind, yet sparked by rage and diffidence, and this is precisely why they work, because it is our pain and suffering, and our awkwardness around it, that so deeply connects us.

The author pulls no punches. We are never cast aside by pretense. We are always invited in. I read a couple of these poems last night before bed and I was surprised where they took me. The only word that accurately describes what I felt is delicious, like something bittersweet that is odd and new, that sustains and lingers. These poems call me back and leave me wanting more. At first it seems as if the author is rambling through his life, a discussion of the past and how the past connects him to his present, but ironically my critical judgment is suspended, when for reasons better known to the poet than to me, I emerge a different person than the one who went in. I am dumbfounded and refreshed. I find myself relaxed and self-assured.

In this energetic age of hand-held devices, instant transmission and video I still find reading most rewarding. And no spoiler alert here because every reader will come away with something different when they read Stan Searl's poems. The abbreviation for Buffalo is BUF and in this work the author is stripped naked, emotionally raw and pure in the Blakean sense, in the buff. He never takes his foot off the accelerator as we drive with him along the treacherous New York State Thruway. Through particulars of love and work in Buffalo the author astonishes the reader with highly imaginative, meditative, provocative and life altering themes.

Lawrence Spann, Ph.D., Poet and Writer

Perfect Submission

Diana became a child who never grew,
who remained—even at seven years old—
a floppy, longish infant,
one with little muscle tone,
unable to sit up by herself,
not crawling or pushing herself around—
totally dependent on her family
for daily life and breath.

I tried to feed her something,
talking to her, encouraging her,
playing with her, being with her,
holding her on my lap then
laying her on the floor with her head
propped up with pillows
as I chattered away,
encouraging her with little blips of sounds,
mostly baby-talk and nonsense noises
to bring us together in that moment,
drinking in time as if there were no time.

It was as if I had regressed
to being a high-school baseball catcher again,
shouting the outs,
directing the team
but here I caught only the air,
throwing back balls to nowhere
yet I pumped out sounds,
my voice bouncing
off the kitchen tiles
to settle into the silence
around the rest of the house,
keeping up my catcher's patter
while the game reeled

onto an invisible field
full of changing forms
as my voice echoed
off the oak moldings
throughout the house
finally, to settle
into stillness and rest.

To Love Diana

felt like plunging beneath the waves of time and space,
diving again and again
like those nesting ospreys in the midst of salt-water creeks,
fierce and insistent as parents,
o*ssifragus*—bone-breakers,
flying out to hunt for fish,
now arriving at the nest with outstretched wings,
coming into the wind,
shrieking their urgency to feed their nestlings,
programmed to love and work together,
whirling and diving into the salt water over and again
to feed their fledglings in the nest.

Swimming with Diana in the Great Peconic Bay

During our ten years in Buffalo,
we rushed to eastern Long Island in the summers,
once renting a dumpy cottage in New Suffolk,
eyeing the crowds at Wickham's Fruit Farm
while we played on the beaches of Cutchogue Harbor.

I placed Diana in a Styrofoam float,
her feet dangling into the salt water
as I swam, pushing her out into the Bay,
so shallow even at high tide,
brought her along on the waves, salt water stinging like spit
keeping her back to gusty south winds.

She floated along on the ruffled waves, flopping her skinny arms,
lifted up out of the salty water coming at us in sheets
as she bobbed, my holding tight to her and the float.

Her arms flailed away
in the push of spray
undulating up and down in the winds,
forced by rough afternoon southerly gusts
to ride atop the waves,
caught and seized by the Bay's wind,
flopping her arms with delight.

Failure and Fire

Diana became like Hephaestus
thrown down from Olympus into an undersea grotto
populated by sea nymphs.
That god had lost his will,
the fall extinguished
all creative fire.

Submerged within the myth,
I realized how our small family
must start a new fire,
mysterious and seemingly impossible.

Maybe ignition could occur under the surface,
an energy source from primal parental instinct,
a form of heart or soul knowing
how my flesh and blood flowed together with Diana,
small, enormous steps might be necessary
so education and learning and hope and love
all mixed up together,
a potent stew with multiple ingredients,
an alchemy from a youthful flame of longing and desire and love.

Song for Julia

The wind howled around the public housing high-rise
kicking up swirls of snow,
pushing at the apartment windows, insistent and noisy
but Julia didn't care about Lake Erie's blowing snow
as she snuggled up in the antique cradle
tucked into heirloom Vermont blankets,
colicky and wide awake for hours and hours.

I cooed, hummed and growled
snatches of cradle songs
supposed to sooth, heal and relax.
Then I had memories
about honey-infused whiskey
used by my grandmother for all pain.

I bundled her up,
tucking in blankets,
sure that only her mouth would be open to the air
as we took the piss-stained elevator
into the drifting storm.
I felt chilled and absurd,
the two of us cuddled up
against Lake Erie's fury
with Julia perfectly still,
a shield to the wind
I ventured outside with her on my chest.

I sang to her again, sotto voce this time,
barely heard against the winds
now non-tunes of harmony,
open-mouthed yet softly voiced
to assure her it was time for sleep.

Back in the apartment,
I peeled off layers,
laid her in the cradle, so carefully,
barely daring to breathe.

More than fifty years later,
those enormous eyes mesmerize,
staring up at me as she started to whoop
a gusto that rings in my ears today.

Our First Buffalo House

Trying to sleep the first night in our house,
I heard steaming and spitting sounds
from the Windshield Wiper plant behind us across Main Street
as the factory wheezed out a clanking cycle
like the crescendo of Harry Partch's Bloboy,
its antique auto horn
blaring through the organ pipes.

Dissonant sounds embraced me,
clanging up and down microtonal scales
bringing an insistent, penetrating message
of welcome to this new, old house
amid the noises of mid-city Buffalo,
oh Buffalo, Buffalo,
my Windshield Wiper Factory, Buffalo.

Quaker First Day School

We sat together in the back rooms of the Buffalo Meetinghouse
to celebrate George Fox and his eccentric *Journal,*
drawing pictures of the top of Pendle Hill and its clouds.

The children used crayons and chalk to walk in his footsteps,
copying bits of text from his *Journal*
filling up multiple pages of drawings
to illustrate—impossible and yet right in front of us—
the man's spirit at work
as he walked up and down the Fells,
with my daughter, Julia, and others
swirling around in chalky colors
as George Fox struggled to the top of Pendle Hill
to experience an ocean of Light and Love
to overcome an ocean of Darkness.

The past leaked into the present.
Densely saturated marks swirled across the paper
as Buffalo's morning light poured into our room,
Julia and others bonding with the pastel drawings
as a Presence filled up their faces,
offerings to the strands of winter light.

Crying Aloud

Once, team teaching,
I found myself bellowing
a cry of pain and anguish
from the great Ahab himself to shout—
"...with a terrific, loud, animal sob,
like that of a heart-stricken moose."

These cries drifted into my heart like bilge-water,
sloshing around, notes of pain tugged,
murmuring how Diana had fused into my flesh.

Dreamlike, a formerly repressed resistance emerged
to urge a rejection of the doctors
who had said they knew better.

I drifted down into a communal harmony,
playing a family music about the end and the beginning,
singing in a newly forming choir
to resist the State and the Experts and the Doctors,
learning a different kind of music,
notes and tunes from the depths of pain and truth.

Citizen Diana

The British research pediatrician said
she's too disabled
that we couldn't manage as a family
because Diana would tear us apart
because Diana belonged in a protected institution
because she would never walk or talk
because West Seneca State School for the Mentally Retarded
would be the perfect place for Diana,
besides, they had a place for her right now.

I knew that Diana's body was small, shrunken and fragile,
now incised and etched upon by this and other doctors
deemed too handicapped
as sterile knives cut into her flesh
onto her chest and forehead
to incise her back and arms and legs
to mark a disabled body
now ready to be placed into the care of New York State,
her previous cuts now dripping bloody flesh,
falling off into the institutional Day Room
where she lay on the large mat,
bits and pieces of her flesh
flaking off around her.

Into the Institution

I hadn't cried like this
since I listened to Kübler-Ross and her radio lecture.
A voice from the grave told her to risk it,
to carry her work with the dying into the future.

I knew that I was a good parent.
I had listened to professional assurances from medical experts,
took in their rational, well-intentioned arguments,
accepted the reality that our child needed too much care, except

all along, it didn't feel at all right.
My head said OK to those expert opinions
but my heart rejected this medical might
even though I understood doctors had dominion.

Even though they said she was much too retarded,
she was my flesh, my soul that I had discarded.

Lost

At first, we couldn't find her at all—so silly
what with the thirty-five children lined up,
Hogg chairs hooked underneath the window sills.
Where then was our Diana child in this long line of hook ups?

It was as if she had disappeared in plain sight,
what with so many other children practically comatose,
tethered together in the enormous day room—a fright
to see heads swollen and disfigured, with most

of the others—unable to keep their heads from a loll—
sprawled together on multiple day room gym mats,
at times writhing in a serpentine crawl—
our child pressed nearly flat to the puke-green wall,

camouflaged by drab, outsized pajamas, cast about
among the other children yet as if separated by a moat.

Adjustment

Kübler-Ross argued that we should embrace the anger and pain
because—eventually—in stages—we must accept the loss—
Diana was too handicapped, would threaten our family, gain
nothing except suffering, ache and more ache.

Although both anger and pain remained real and profound,
we would find that we probably did the right thing
placing our tiny sick child inside institutional grounds
because experts knew better, had their rationale for being.

Why shouldn't we move through this stage of grief
become more reasonable, like good parents, of course?
We did the right thing—absolutely—for our child's brief
sojourn on earth, listening to experts and their diplomas.

Even today, I admire Kübler-Ross's work on each stage—
so why do I still simmer with such doubt and rage?

No Clothes

We never got over how the place lost all of Diana's clothes
the ones my wife had labeled—over days and days with care—
shirts, pants and dresses with Diana's name stitched in rows.
Yet, institutional appetite had devoured everything—unaware,

erased the last trace of identity, lost her clothes.
For the six months she lived in the state institution
part of her disappeared, even when we visited—those
oversized clothes swallowed her tiny constitution.

If they couldn't track her name, her basic identity
what chance did she have to get what she needed?
Was it better to let go, turn her into a nobody?
How could we take her home …we couldn't really succeed?

Blasted by Lake Erie's winds, anger swelled in a flood
rising up like enormous waves churning through the blood.

Identity Politics

At times, seizures carried Diana away,
her body trembled,
shaking as if powered by an underground source
as we rushed her to a hospital.

Her body writhed and gave off
a message that children like this one cannot
be managed and require care from the State.
It's not fair to parents.
The best thing for everyone
is to be realistic and to realize
this child should be discarded.

Yet, her flesh was my flesh,
this daughter named for the Virgin goddess huntress,
triple goddess of witchcraft and mystery.

Artemis, goddess of chaste yearnings,
help this family in our time of great need,
Protect us and guide us
in a spiritual awakening
even in the midst of loss and despair—
challenge our family
to honor her name, Diana,
beloved and perfect and pure.

Institutional Air

Lake-effect snow squalls blinded us
as we drove through the West Seneca State School complex,
low residential buildings squatted in the blowing snow,
drifts skittering around the roadway
to obscure most of the entrances,
dream-like openings through these snowy eddies.

I found myself crawling down a hallway
unable to walk upright
my nose and mouth accosted by urine and chlorine smells,
nose-clamping odor difficult to breathe,
the tangy bitterness of wet diapers
mixed with moist feces
children piled-up around the edge of an enormous day-room,
arranged in special chairs around the outside,
other spaces filled-up with squirming infants
writhing together on the floor.

I heard underground, flute-like sounds,
imagining a grinning, goat-like Pan figure,
a music of rumbling, plucked bass notes
pumping harsh animal cries,
pulsations of a fiercely insistent rhythm
like the yips from an overheated beast,
caught and seized in a recently sprung trap.

I tried to rise
but bent my ear to a low wall,
absorbed by low cries of longing—
was it really human noises
coming out of the trapped ones,
now sounding like a sustained drone?

I heard it as an out-of-tune
crying out and tortured animal,
calling to me about Diana
who sang to me in a choral-like voice,
released into the
acrid air of the day room.

The Sunshine Fund

The sun never appeared
when we drove out there each year.

We met with the Director and his staff,
handing-out toys and dolls as well as a check
to bring our parental sunshine
into the midst of this New York State Institution,
formerly the State Institution for Feeble-Minded Children,
then the New York State Custodial Asylum for Feeble-Minded
Women of Child-Bearing Age.

Even though I had a full beard,
I wasn't at Newark as a Santa Claus
but as a laggard elf who worked underground,
connected to the snow- spitting clouds
that fit perfectly into this latest disguise
hands that offered toys and gifts from an engorged heart,
one that swelled with rage
yet kept it all together even in the Director's office.

Yet, underneath it all, joining the icy crystals
facing directly into the force of the full-bloom gusts,
I imagined how to bring these offerings into the Institution itself,
conjuring up blowing, drifting ice without the touch of sunshine
to bring these bone-chilling snow showers
like icy breath from an evil sorcerer
to freeze the Director and his entire staff
right there in the office,
everything now enclosed
become ice sculptures in the drifting snow
that entered the Newark State School for the Mentally Retarded,
cold and dead and terrible.

Singing in the Institution

I've never heard the likes of such singing, such weeping.
Oh, I don't know, I just don't know.
It was Christmas time and bells were ringing.

Tears flooded down from our Schola Cantoum singers.
Oh, I don't know, I just don't know.
I've never heard the likes of such singing, such weeping.

The retarded adults loved to hear this singing
as tears flooded down from our Schola Cantoum singers.
It was Christmas time and bells were ringing.

Disabled bodies groaned with the heart and soul of singing.
Oh, I don't know, I just don't know.
I've never heard the likes of such singing, such weeping.

In this circle of moaning, residents were creeping
to embrace the singers, open to a different kind of knowing.
It was Christmas time and bells were ringing.

These professional singers lost themselves with sobbing,
absorbing a moment as if they could feel another knowing.
I've never heard the likes of such singing, such weeping.
It was Christmas time and bells were ringing.

Pushing Back

I took the Older Women's League motto to heart,
"Don't Agonize; Organize"
into committees, Boards of Directors,
meeting the Director of West Seneca State School,
active on the Community Services Board of that place
a perfect model of a rational, good parent
to urge more funding for community alternatives,
testifying before the Erie County Health Committee,
even starting an institutional parent chapter
of the State Association for Retarded Children.

Yet, under the surface,
hallucinations swarmed my mind and heart,
filled with the plight of Heracles
imagining his second terrible, heroic Labor
where—only with Athena's immediate presence
did he slay Hydra's terrible heads,
burying the ninth, immortal one,
an urge came over me
during one of the visits to my daughter.

I pulled up next to the Administration Building,
starting to burrow into the soil
underneath the Director's office at the State School
to break through the concrete foundation,
dug and dug underneath the building,
taking the ninth and immortal head of the Hydra
from the station wagon's junky way-back,
sensing Athena in my ear,
Oh dig right here, she said,
make sure you bury it deep and clear right here.

Dreaming Apples

It was the light,
scattered unevenly within the apple tree branches,
reflected over the green and reddish surfaces like a watercolor,
a softness, lovely and perfect
yet in the midst of change.
I longed for Diana to join this fruity orchard light,
pruning, picking together.

I dreamed crunchy Macoun apples,
so crisp and sharp and sweet all-at-once—
surely Diana would like to bite into these perfect apples,
what with richly layered sweetness
pouring out into her from the entire orchard
mixed-up with sluggish wasps,
feeling the October sun on her white-as-snow skin,
the light shifting into the afternoon between the rows of trees
opening up to the orchard's roots
the Jonagolds splayed off into the south edges of the farm road
remembering walking with Diana
into bright but not quite warm October sunshine
with her bundled up on the chest
as I sat right there in our Elam Place home,
trying to disguise the carrots and peas within Mott's applesauce
as I battled her odd hypoglycemia
praying that the applesauce and orange juice
might sidestep her failed metabolism.

Singing with the Buffalo Quakers

Some Sunday mornings
we arrived early
to sing hymns together.

Diana sat on my lap when I played the piano,
thumping away at the keyboard,
her thin, delicate reddish tinged hair
glowing as we moved into silent worship,
flapping her hands at first
but then settled into the silent waiting,
absorbed in group prayer of listening.

Relaxed, her floppy head lulled over
while I heard echoes of the hymn tunes play within me,
more and more relaxed with her on my lap,
hoping that I wouldn't fall asleep and start
to snore as we sat there
all together in a gathering stillness
to draw into a unity,
Diana resting on my chest,
breathing with me through the silence,
whole and complete.

I mouthed but didn't sing aloud
"Now Thank We All our God,"
its music the space inside my rising and falling
breathing with Diana.

Parental Secrets

An osprey flew into my mind,
spreading out its six-foot wing span
to enter my skull with shrill trills
as it reached the platform on the telephone-pole nest
in the midst of our salt-meadow wetlands,
the wind harsh from the east
as salt water poured into submerged sawgrass
beneath the screeching into its nest
to feed its young with parts of an enormous blue-fish.

Introduced anew from the wetlands outside Buffalo,
this osprey pair
started over again after the DDT ban,
the ospreys resurrected in our own backyard
now calling to my heart,
coming back at the same time every March,
coupled for life
now turning into the stiff, cold spring winds,
how these parents flew over the farm dikes
into the middle of Wickham's Creek
pushed by the persistent easterly gusts
to feed their young,
protective and secure atop the nests
calling with their high-pitched whistling.

In Memory of Burton Blatt

Founder of the Center on Human Policy at Syracuse University

We sat in Dean Blatt's office at Syracuse
pouring out woe
how we placed our child in the institution,
how Diana had disappeared in the bowels of the State School,
how we had lost her
as if she were already dead,
anger and hopelessness all wrapped up together.

I remember
how Burton Blatt said
go see Fred Finn
at Seaside Regional Center in Connecticut,
tell him I sent you …
see for yourselves
what good programs can do
for children like Diana.

Even though he died young,
Blatt sung his own cracked,
broken Jewish wisdom songs
celebrating plain speaking,
cutting through ordinary bullshit,
flinging insults,
trying to help us to learn
to love one another.

Singing with Artemis

In mid-June, a full moon rose over the Great Peconic Bay
like a stairway to Artemis herself, shimmering rungs bending,
reaching across the Cutchogue harbor on its way
into the center of the evening's ending.

The moonlight's trench created
a wave-tipped shadowy passageway
to illuminate some hidden source unabated,
dependent on mystery, yet an invisible gateway

where shards of light pierced the oncoming darkness.
I ached to ride upon those reflected beams
as if catching a sweet fragrance of rightness,
to swing together with my own Diana, redeemed,

propelled by the goddess and her dance of light.
She whispered to me from beyond my mortal sight.

Buffalo Hands

for Anne Scattergood Fogg

Those cooking hands,
pulling together suppers out of nothing
where her fingers worked together in perfect harmony,
cooking as easy improvisation,
cutting up carrots and broccoli
to pick through ratty lettuces, slicing onions
like tossing together a popular song,
always in a simple key like C or G
harmonious, as if she
didn't have a care in the world.

Her hands drifted
into my mind to recall
a time together in Buffalo
where we visited potential public schools
for daughter, Julia, observing fifth grade classrooms.

This Quaker woman chanted
another tune and I found myself
floating out with her
as she carried on and laughed saying
"Oh this is not for Julia,
she needs that special rigor and creativity …
let's keep looking, shall we?"
Her hands directing,
fingers pointing ahead,
the hands opening and closing,
to tap-tap a rhythm of the next song.

She insisted that Julia sing in her own way
open to a music of the heart,
not forced yet reeling down to the soul
to join a deeper, inner harmony
speaking joy and thanksgiving in learning.

Traveling Home

Our junky red Ford wagon
bumped along the Thruway's concrete ridges for hundreds of miles
as we sang the Erie Canal song
"We had an old mule and her name is Sal
fifteen miles on the Erie Canal"
over and over next to the locks,
driving the Thruway from Buffalo to Albany
hugging the canal at times,
trying to get from Buffalo to Cutchogue
on eastern Long Island over five hundred miles away.

In the midst of a return to Buffalo,
deep into the Thruway night
with Julia asleep and Diana in the institution,
we drove west of Syracuse
smelling the thick, black dirt of the onion fields to the north,
then the National Wildlife refuge on both sides of the road,
meditating about Diana,
we realized an odd thing that
either we were crazy and should simply hide our heads
or that the Institution—the State of New York
was insane and we were the sane ones.

As the outside darkness closed upon the car
the concrete thumping under us,
it came to us nearly as a dream
that Diana was a real person.

Our bones vibrated into the Thruway.
We chanted how much Diana mattered
that we needed her as she needed us,
thumping into the late Thruway night,
the cement grooves like a ground-bass,
playing this urgent message into our vibrating hearts.

Our New Day Center Program

Once every five years or so,
The New York Times investigates institutional abuse and neglect.

It's always the same:
staff called the inmates "retard" and "idiot"
residents soak in their own piss and shit
as if we had entered an undersea grotto,
one in which Thetis provided a secret cave
where we stepped into a swirling flow
from a tidal force
beneath the surface of language.

Pushed by this salty source
as the tide flowed in,
carrying all in its powerful wake,
hidden yet in plain sight as
we started our church-basement program
for Diana and a couple of kids like her.

A social worker from the State Institution
referred parents to us—
even at the austere Children's Rehabilitation Center
a different social worker referred parents to us as well
to help us to develop a school for Diana
as well as other medically fragile,
profoundly handicapped kids
who needed an educational program.

Springville

Lake effect snow dumped onto the Boston Hills,
westerly winds pushing across
to pummel our reliable Ford Falcon
as it chugged up to our rented brick farmhouse,
snow curling sculptured drifts from Lake Erie's squalls.

Day after day the same,
the snow spit-out clots
pushing at the old car
as I drove back and forth to Buffalo,
thirty-five miles away, taking Diana
to school after Julia's bus
brought her to an open classroom in Springville.

Mostly, Julia played games, working with clay,
drawing and reading a little
but not really learning math
as the winds pressed on around the farmhouse.

I breathed into these stiff winds
to greet Julia as we struggled,
winds sweeping down the hill
as Lake Erie itself drifted in around us.

The year Diana died
the snow swirled around the Thruway
then followed us up the hill.

The Boston Hills

Going back and forth to Buffalo that fall and winter,
I counted twenty-three days in a row
during November and December
when the sun didn't shine—
not for a single second—
the weather cloudy and lowering skies
to spit out dirty ice and snow
as the *Buffalo Evening News* quoted John Barth
who said it's perfect weather
for a writer of Gothic novels.

In early November,
visiting friends as we did often on the weekend,
we had a call that
Diana had been taken to the hospital.

When I called Children's Hospital,
the nurses said they did not have a patient named Diana
that we needed to call her doctor.

We sat together with friends.
I kept calling and calling,
trying to locate Diana in her hospital room then
—finally—
someone put her doctor on the phone
oh Mr. Searl I'm so sorry …
Diana died earlier this morning.

A Quaker Memorial Worship

One Buffalo Quaker quoted first Corinthians how
'It's only love that guides our voices today
because as Corinthians says
'If I have the gift of prophecy
and can fathom all mysteries
and all knowledge,
and if I have a faith
that can move mountains,
but do not have love,
I am nothing.'

The speaker insisted
'love never fails—
people needed to listen
to Diana's family and to her life—
her loss is a deep rent in our community.'

A young man said
he loved to see her in our worship meeting
as she looked around at us,
sitting in her mother's lap,
flapping her arms at times,
perfectly contented in our silence.
Thank you, God, for her life
without sin or blemish,
perfect in every way
in the sight of Divine Presence.

Another speaker remembered Isaiah
how a little child will lead us.

Isn't this a great mystery after all
as we open to the influence of the Spirit in our lives?
As we remember her life,
isn't it fit to recall our own faith
and how we continue to remain, open,
expectant, breathing in the Divine together?

Diana's School Today

The chalkboard in the entrance
said welcome Mr. Stan, one of the founders
as I toured the Center for Handicapped Children in Buffalo,
a school that we started in the early 70's
now populated by over fifty students.

I walked into the classrooms and the gym,
musing about beginnings and endings,
how Diana—fragile, delicate and vulnerable—
flowed into this present moment
in the midst of trauma, pain and sorrow.

Walking out to my rental car,
I recalled the fiercely protective ospreys,
shrieking their hunting calls over the salt meadow,
determined to come back to the nest and feed their young,

protected by a persistent love
those swooping ospreys sailing over salt meadows,
the mind reeling and dropping into the water,
hopeful and alive in the cycle of life and death.

A Fierce Love

Why can't love be as fierce,
penetrating and powerfully physical
as working on the Pipe Crew
for Perini Construction building Route 91?

We young men shoveled Vermont's rocky soil,
leaning into the digging—
our bodies sunk into breaking up dirt,
persistent, swinging shovels
like baseball bats at times,
bodies projected into crusty, pebble-strewn soil,
absorbed in the moment of scratching and digging
a frenzy of physical desire,
sweating and attacking
until we had trenched into the earth.

I dug the hard-packed earth
next to Diana's granite marker
in back of the Cutchogue Methodist Church's cemetery,
scraping the stubborn sandy soil
to prepare a suitable place
to bury her ashes.
My hands and upper arms trembled,
recalling my construction days
as I deposited Diana's
burnt up bones into the ground.

Because of an early hurricane,
the lilacs bloomed that September,
splashy with colors and new life.

Special Thanks

I appreciate the professional critiques and recommendations about this manuscript from Candelin Wahl, Co-Editor of the *Mud Season Review* and David Rigsbee, American poet and critic. In addition, I appreciate the detailed editorial suggestions from William Wallis, teacher, poet and mentor. These recommendations mattered; thank you all.

Also, I have had continued encouragement, critique and support from our local poetry gathering in Culver City, including Rachel Fretz, Ruth Gooley, Lorreta Heiser and William Walllis.

Finally, thank you to Janice C. Gentz, Executive Director of the CHC Learning Center, a Program of the Center for Handicapped Children, Inc. on Eggert Road in Amherst, New York. Jan and her staff have extended the educational program that we started for my daughter, Diana Margaret Searl, born April 8, 1967 in Syracuse, New York and died on November 10, 1974 in Buffalo.

About the Author

Stanford Searl lives in Culver City, California with his wife, Rebecca Warren Searl. He has a Ph.D. in English from Syracuse University and taught at Buffalo State University College in the 1970's. For twenty-five years, Searl was a Core Faculty member of an interdisciplinary and learner-centered doctoral program at Union Institute & University and later an English Instructor for the Los Angeles Community Colleges.

In 2005, Searl published two non-fiction books about Quaker silent worship, including *Voices from the Silence* and *The Meanings of Silence in Quaker Worship*. In 2014, he published *Quaker Poems: The Heart Opened* and in 2016 he published *Homage to the Lady with the Dirty Feet and other Vermont Poems*. *Songs for Diana* is his third book of poems and he is completing a poetry chapbook about Mary Dyer and other Quaker prophets and martyrs who were hanged in Boston, Massachusetts in the middle of the 17th century.